SCOTTISH AIRS AND DANCES FOR TWO VIOLINS (OR SOLO VIOLIN)

GUITAR CHORDS INCLUDED
MB22250
BY ANNE WITT

Visit us on the Web at www.melbay.com or www.billsmusicshelf.com

ABOUT SCOTTISH AIRS AND DANCES

The twenty-five pieces in this collection date back to eighteenth and nineteenth century Scotland. Music was passed around among professional and amateur musicians, hand copied, and ended up in slightly different versions in many collections. The Airs were originally songs or for solo violin. The Dances - strathspeys, reels, jigs, a hornpipe, and the sword dance - were originally for fiddle or bagpipe. The book is arranged as a program from beginning to end - from sunrise, with *"Ossians's Hymn to the Sun,"* to sunset, with the lullaby *"O, Can Ye Sew Cushions."* And no Scottish evening is complete without *"Auld Lang Syne"* as a finale. But one can, of course, choose to play a selection.

Three of the airs are Gaelic songs. Others are tunes for which Robert Burns and other poets wrote lyrics. Two airs were composed for the violin - *"Neil Gow's Lament for the Death of His Second Wife"* and the anonymous *"Killiecrankie,."* The dances were played by fiddlers or pipers. They played (and still play) many of the same pieces. One example is *"Gillie Callum,"* the sword dance. Originally a bagpipe tune, its range was expanded beyond the pipes' nine notes and it became a fiddle tune.

The composers are anonymous except for pieces by Niel Gow (1727-1807), his son, Nathaniel Gow (1763-1831) and William Marshall (1748-1833). Niel Gow was the preeminent violinist of his day. All three composed many fiddle tunes for Scottish country dancing.

Most of the pieces are presented in sets of two, and they should be played without stopping in-between, as they would be performed at a country dance. Metronome markings are given as a guideline. Guitar chords are included ad libitum. Since the first violin generally has the melody, the pieces can also be played by solo violin.

The music of Scotland is unique. The airs have their own special beauty. The dances are fun to play, with lively tempos, dotted rhythms and sudden key changes. This music has long been the pleasure of country fiddlers and pipers. These new arrangements for two violins are perfect for student and teacher as well as violin colleagues.

Anne Witt

Contents

Ossian's Hymn to the Sun

(Laoidh Oisein Do'n Ghrian)

Gaelic Air ♩. = 63

Arranged by Anne Witt

Wantonness

Arranged by Anne Witt

Steer Her Up and Had Her Gawn

Arranged by Anne Witt

Jamie Come Try Me

Slow Air ♩ = 72

Arranged by Anne Witt

Ye Shepherds

Arranged by Anne Witt

The Banks of Doon

Arranged by Anne Witt

Gillie Callum

Sword dance - moderate ♩ = 108

Arranged by Anne Witt

Gloomy Winter

Arranged by Anne Witt

Strathspey - moderate ♩ = 100

Whistle an' I'll come to ye, my love

Arranged by Anne Witt

Logan Water

Air ♩ = 76

Arranged by Anne Witt

The Haughs* of Cromdale

Arranged by Anne Witt

Strathspey - Moderate ♩ = 108

slide on the beat

*Scots dialect for meadows.

Neil Gow's Lament for the Death of His Second Wife

Niel Gow (1727-1807)
Arranged by Anne Witt

2nd violin should play a bit softer than first.

I Ha'e a Wife o' my Ain

Arranged by Anne Witt

If played more than once, 1st and 2nd violin can switch parts.

Killiecrankie

Arranged by Anne Witt

To make this a violin solo piece, the 1st violin should play the opening 2nd violin part.

Jenny's Lamentation

Arranged by Anne Witt

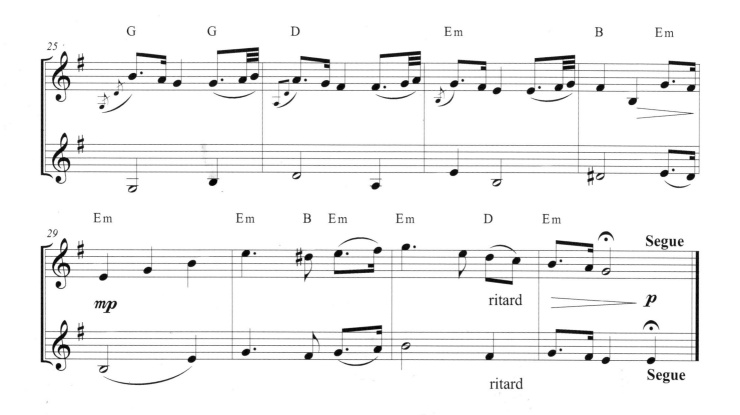

Alas for me

(Oich Mar Tha Mi)

Gaelic Air ♩ = 96

Arranged by Anne Witt

Miss Admiral Gordon's Strathspey

Wm. Marshall (1748-1833)
Arranged by AnneWitt

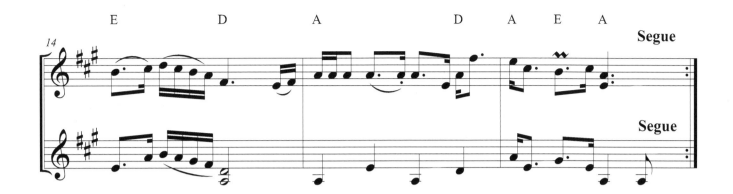

Lady Glenorchy

Reel ♩ = 72

Arranged by Anne Witt

Lady Charlotte Campbell

Nathaniel Gow (1763-1831)
Arranged by Anne Witt

A Hundred Pipers

Jig ♩. = 104

Arranged by Anne Witt

Loch Torridon

Arranged by Anne Witt

Muirland Willie

Arranged by Anne Witt

The Lay of Fraoch
(Laiodh Fraioch)

Arranged by Anne Witt

Gaelic Air - play in slow 2/4 ♩ = 52   Use very little vibrato.

O, Can Ye Sew Cushions

Arranged by Anne Witt

Auld Lang Syne

Air ♩ = 88

Arranged by Anne Witt

Notes

Ossian (p. 4) was the creation of James Macpherson (1736-1796), a Scottish school teacher. MacPherson purportedly found fragments of ancient Gaelic texts written by an old blind bard of the third century named Ossian (Oisein in Gaelic). MacPherson published these fragments from 1760 to 1775. They include visions of battles long ago set in wild, vague landscapes of mountain and sea, and stories of dead heroes like Fingal and Uillin who dwelt in the clouds. The romantic and melancholy atmosphere evoked in the Ossianic poems and songs caught like wildfire with the public. The books of Ossian became bestsellers in Britain and Europe and, though fake, they showed that MacPherson had talent, and his Ossian was admired by writers like Thomas Gray, Chateaubriand, and Goethe.

Gillie Callum (p.11) is the famous dance done by men in kilts over crossed swords laid on the ground after victory in battle. Today it is an exhibition dance done by male or female dancers. In Gaelic, gillie means lad, and Callum is a male name. Gillie also denotes a male servant. Like many anonymous old tunes Gillie Callum can be found in slightly different versions. The tune is played on the bagpipe and fiddle.

A *strathspey* (p. 12 et al.) is a Scottish dance that today is usually done in a moderate tempo. The dance is done by groups of two or more couples in intricate patterns. The music is in 4/4 time and is particularly known for its dotted note patterns of long-short, long-short, with the occasional short-long, which is called the Scottish snap.

Niel Gow (1727-1807) (p. 16) was the preeminent Scottish fiddler of his day. His style of playing reportedly changed the nature of fiddling. He was famous throughout Scotland and performed for the aristocracy. His portrait was painted by Sir Henry Raeburn who painted society and intellectual luminaries of Scotland. Gow composed many tunes for violin which were published by his son, Nathaniel (see below).

Killiecrankie (p. 18) was the site of a famous battle on July 17, 1689, between the Jacobites who were the Scottish followers of the exiled James III (Jacob being Latin for James) and the Scottish Whigs who, along with the English, supported King William and Queen Mary. The Jacobites won the battle that day, but the cause was lost until renewed in 1745 by Bonnie Prince Charlie. The tune, Killiecrankie, though written in a predominantly major key has a wistful feeling to it.

William Marshall (1748-1833) (p. 22) was a renowned fiddler and composer. He wrote more than 250 dance tunes and airs many of which are still popular today He earned his living as a butler for the Duke of Gordon and rose to become manager of the Duke's estates. He published two collections of tunes during his lifetime and a third collection appeared posthumously.

Nathaniel Gow (1763-1831) (p. 24) was the most successful of Niel Gow's sons, four of whom became professional fiddlers. He entered the music publishing business, publishing his father's compositions and his own which are included in six volumes entitled *Collections of Strathspey Reels*. He also published the four volume *Complete Repository of the Original Scotch Slow Tunes*.

About the Arranger

Anne Witt began playing the viola as a child, always preferring its distinctly mellow tone. She studied art and music at Goucher College and has played in orchestras, chamber ensembles, and string quartets over many years. She took up the bagpipe as an adult and performs regularly as a soloist at ceremonial events near her home. An interest in Scottish fiddle music prompted her to begin arranging fiddle tunes for viola. She has also published *Scottish Fiddling for Viola* (Mel Bay).

The Lay of Fraoch

(from the Gaelic original)

Fever's languor overcame Eochaidh's* daughter, *E-och-i
  he, Chief of the Brimming Horns.
She sent the news to Fraoch.
  That hero asked what would she?

Back her answer came: The only cure –
  her soft white palms full of rowan fruit from Lodain pool
  and only Fraoch to seek for them.

"Fruit I never gathered," answered Fraoch MacIdhaidh, the warrior.
  "But tho' never here-to-fore,
  yet will I pluck the fruit for Mhaibh.*" *Maive

So away he hied, and, swimming gracefully the deep loch,
  he found the Monster in sleep
  and its mouth close to the rowans.

22468107R00020

Printed in Great Britain
by Amazon